FOLLOW UP

Category: Business & Economics

Description: Remove all hope for competitors.

Key words: Follow up

Copyright Bob Oros-2017

ISBN 978-1-105-22544-4

Written and published by Bob Oros

FOLLOW UP	1
Follow up Remove all hope for competitors	5
How many sales people follow up	5
Why you lose business	6
What your customers want	14
Be impressed	20
Any mail today	21
Do they want to see you	22
Be specific	23
Ask for help	24
People always conform	25
Personal interests	26
Important dates	27
Ask for advice	28

Your approach to problems 29

Follow up: Remove all hope for competitors 33

My 4% improvement objective: 35

What the entire book series will do for you 37

Ben Franklin's system 38

Achieve a 52% improvement 43

Follow up
Remove all hope for competitors

How many sales people follow up

Only 10% of sales people follow up to a buyers complete satisfaction. Do I know what my customer expects after the sale? No matter how hard you worked or how much you have discounted your price when you sell a customer, he or she then feels that you still owe them something. The perception on the part of the customer is that you, the seller, have not only gotten new business but also his or her money. There were many other sales people after the same account and the same business but you were chosen as the recipient.

Therefore, psychologically, you now owe your customer a favor. Even though you had to bend over backwards to get the order. That is why follow up is so important to keeping the business.

We have been calling on a particular customer for months and have never gotten to first base. They are polite, however, they keep telling us to come back at a later date. All of a sudden we make a small sale!

As soon as we leave the account we check the stock status. Everything is checked and you drop a card in the mail that your customer receives the next morning confirming the order, delivery date and approximate delivery time. After we check to be sure everything was delivered we make a follow up call to be sure everything was alright with the product. We get a few small reorders and continue the same follow up strategies. And then the orders get larger. Soon we are the primary supplier. Later we are having lunch with the customer and he lets us in on the reason he switched: YOU FOLLOWED UP AND YOUR COMPETITOR DID NOT !

Why you lose business

In a study done by the Small Business Administration they asked business owners why they felt customers stopped buying. Nearly all said their prices were too high. But when the agency surveyed the customers of these people to find out the real reason they left, here is what they found:

  2%   died
  3%   moved away
  9%   cited price
14%   dissatisfied with the product
68%   felt their business was not appreciated

Think of it! Over half left because no one said thank you!

The agency also determined that it cost 6 times more to attract a new customer than it does to keep an existing customer!

What is the easiest way for a competitor to take a customer away from you? Why do you lose accounts to your competitors?

Here are some reasons that sound good: Our service isn't up to par. Our prices are too high. We have too many out-of-stocks. My competitor is better known in my market.

I have a surprise for you. When you lose an account it is mostly due to one reason. I would say that 95% of all the accounts you lose to a competitor are for this single reason! This single reason will enable you to take away more business from your competitor than you can handle.

It's easier than you think. Here's why. Your competitors are taking their customers for granted. I guarantee it! Let me say that again in capital letters...

YOUR COMPETITORS ARE TAKING THEIR CUSTOMERS FOR GRANTED.

And do you know what else? So are you - I know, I know - you don't want to hear that. It's true - you know it and I know it.

Let's put it to the test. Do you feel appreciated? Probably not. Would you like a little appreciation? If your answer is yes - you are not alone. In a recent survey 6,600 people were asked two questions:

1. Do you receive as much praise, recognition and appreciation as you feel you deserve?

6,415 SAID NO

2. Would you perform your job better if you were given more praise, recognition and appreciation?

6,495 SAID YES

This, of course, doesn't apply to you - you are in sales - it is up to you to GIVE appreciation not GET it. The point is - most people feel unappreciated.

Here's more proof - a real life example: I was helping a small distributor look for a way to promote their business. We thought about a trade show, however, due to the small size of the company we felt that it would be too big of an undertaking. After a lot of talking we finally came up with a program we called a "customer appreciation dinner."

We contacted 20 of his suppliers and asked them to participate by serving dinner to the customers and at the same giving them the opportunity to show samples of their products. All the suppliers agreed and we put together a buffet line concept with the theme being that we want to show our customers that we appreciate their business.

We decided to use an RSVP format so we would know how many people would show up, and we could tell the suppliers how many people they could plan on feeding. We arranged to have the dinner at a Holiday Inn with a room large enough to hold 108 people at one time.

We sent out 525 invitations expecting to get about 200 RSVP's. The invitation said, "When was the last time someone took you to dinner to show you how much they appreciate your business?"

Not knowing the power of our theme, "Customer Appreciation Dinner", we had 525 RSVP's! We had to turn the tables FIVE TIMES during the evening. Every restaurant in the small southern town was closed with a sign on the door saying "Closed - we went out for dinner."

The normal procedure is to get an account, wine and dine them during the honeymoon period, and then put them on auto pilot. You are guilty of it, aren't you? Admit it.

How can you take away business from a competitor? Here's the secret. Get a small order from your competitor's customer and then show that you REALLY appreciate their business. Too simple? - You WILL stand out and be noticed.

Sure, you gave the customer a discount - THEY should appreciate YOU! Your customer is the one who writes out those big checks every week - they are not thinking about how much they appreciate the small discount they got - they are wondering if YOU appreciate the amount of business THEY are giving YOU.

Your customers pay your mortgage, put your kids through school, make your car payments, pay for your retirement plan. Your top twenty customers - Do you thank them enough? Do you show them that you appreciate their business? More than likely the answer is no.

Give your customers the attention and appreciation they are hungry for. Give your prospects the attention and appreciation they are not getting from their current supplier and you will take away the business.

Few things are more gratifying than gratitude, and very few sales people express their gratitude as much as they should.

Appreciation can go a lot farther than just saying thank you. How many thank you notes did you send last year? Your competitors are not doing it. It's the little messages of gratitude that will make a big difference.

I was sitting in a buyer's office when a fax came in for him. He seemed a little upset so I asked him if there was anything wrong. He said a salesman had just left with a large order and he just faxed a thank you note.

I thought that was pretty good for a sales person to take the time to send a thank you fax. However, the buyer said he was going to cancel the order, but because of the thank you note it became too difficult to call and cancel.

You never know what insurance your thank you notes, follow up phone calls and extra attention is providing. Here is more proof.

Headquarters wanted to know why a small pizza shop was performing way beyond everyone's expectations. They were number one in a large national chain – yet located in a small town with a lot of competition. When they investigated they found that before closing they would go through their deliveries and call everyone to make sure their pizza was good!

CAN YOU IMAGINE THAT? A thank you call from a PIZZA SHOP?

I just bought a new house. After the closing I never heard a peep from the broker - nothing - zero! I even had to call his office and tell them to come and get their sign out of my yard!

No - Service is not the reason you lose business.

No - Price is not the reason you lose business.

No - Your competitor's image in the market is not the reason.

No - it's none of those things.

The reason you lose, on average TWENTY-FIVE PERCENT OF YOUR BUSINESS EVERY YEAR is because you didn't listen to your mother when she told you to say "Thank You."

What your customers want

What are the things customers want from a sales person? The only way to know for certain is to ask them. I did just that and here is what they told me.

1. "Do not sell me - help me buy. Give me a choice between something I want and something else I want and help me decide what is best. Do not try to push something on me just because you want to sell it."

One of the things buyers really dislike is a pushy sales person. There is no faster way to damage the relationship than to apply too much pressure on your customer. Our job is to sell, however, business to business selling is much different than the "one call close" type of selling. During a one call close presentation the sales person knows that once he or she walk out the door of the prospects home the sale has ended. Many of the sales training programs we encounter are designed on this type of selling, as are many of the books we read about selling. There is a big difference.

2. "Do not sound like you just graduated from selling 101. Do not use timeworn techniques to pressure me to buy when I do not want to. Sound like someone trying to help me. Sound like a friend."

Again, we must set aside many of the basic selling tactics used in consumer selling. For example; the use of a "tie down" question. Here is how it works. A customer asks you if the product comes in a number 10 can. You respond with: "would you like it in a number 10 can?"

This response makes you sound like an amateur. How should you respond? "Yes Bill, this does come in a number 10 can. It also comes in a plastic pouch. Would either one of those work out for you?" Only a slight difference, however, the first response implies pressure without having all the facts, while the second response implies that you are interested in helping them make the best choice.

3. "Be sincerely interested in what I do. My business may not seem overly impressive to you, but it is everything to me. Be interested enough in my problems to ask questions and help me find solutions."

The old school of selling used to teach us to have a high self interest. I remember one training school I attended where the instructor told me to visualize "My money is in the customer's wallet - my job is to get it!" That works well when making a one time sale, however, that type of attitude will destroy a relationship as well as a career in sales that require long term relationships. It is up to you to know the difference.

4. "Do not talk down to me or tell me what I am doing is wrong. I want to feel good about the choices I have made. If I have made a mistake, be tactful. Show me how others have made the same mistake."

This desire on the part of the customer is simply to deal with a sales person who is considerate and tactful. No one likes to make a mistake; however, if you have never made any mistakes you have never done anything worthwhile. When pointing out a mistake that a customer is making, do it with extreme tact.

5. "Reinforce my decision to buy from you. I need to be reassured that buying products and services is my best alternative. Do not take my business for granted - let me know I am appreciated."

We are all guilty of taking our best customers for granted. Once a customer has been buying from us we have a tendency to let up and take it easy. We forget that our competitors are calling on them and giving them the attention they crave. If we take our customer for granted we are very likely going to be left out in the cold.

6. "Do not tell me - show me how you will service me after I commit to writing checks totaling thousands of dollars every month. Do not forget me after the initial sale by putting me on automatic pilot."

There is an old saying that is very applicable to today's business: "What you do speaks so loudly I cannot hear what you say." Empty promises and good intentions simply do not keep the business. Even if you have a good relationship with the customer it can dissolve in a heartbeat if you do not take care of their needs and help them achieve their goals.

"Tell me success stories. Tell me about similar situations where someone using your products and services is having success. I do not want to be the first or the only. I will have a lot more confidence if I know of others who purchased and are doing well."

Once we make a sale the job is only beginning. We have to keep our customers sold and this requires reselling them every week. Talk about the successes people are having with your products and your company. When you or someone in your company opens a new account, do not keep it a secret. Customers like to deal with someone who is successful.

7. "Give me proof. I want to believe what you say, however, I have heard it all. I need facts and information that back up the statements you make. Show me a letter from a satisfied customer. I want reassurance and justification the price I am paying is fair for what I am buying."

Always back up your statements and claims with proof. When presenting new products do the required homework. Get the facts and figures to back up everything you say. Do not just rely on your relationship with the customer to make the sale. Show them you care enough to do the homework.

Following are a few things you can do to build your relationship:

Be impressed

The first lesson in selling to a business is to realize that there are no such things as companies, only people. You don't sell your products to some inanimate organization that makes rational decisions based on logical data. You sell to a human, emotional, somewhat irrational person who makes the decision based on issues of ego, personality and irrationality. With this in mind you have to use the same basic principle you use to win anyone over to your way of thinking. The person you are dealing with has to like you and think you know what you are talking about before they will listen to anything you have to say.

The best way to impress your customer is to let the other person know, in a sincere way, that you think he or she is really special. Tell them what great work they do or what a fantastic business they have.

Find something you have in common. People like people who are like them. And people believe and trust people they like. Try to discover attitudes, likes, dislikes, family backgrounds, experiences, personality virtues or quirks, careers, goals, or values that you have in common with others; then emphasize them. People reason that if you're like them in some ways, you're probably like them in other ways. Therefore, they begin to transfer trust as friend to friend.

Any mail today

People like to receive mail, especially if it something personal. The first thing people do when they get home is check the mail. The same is true at the office.

The mail is normally sorted out by importance with some never even being opened. However, a short personal note or a card of some type is always appreciated and sends a signal that they have not been forgotten. It can be anything from a news item in a trade journal to a cartoon that would be appropriate.

This has become so important that there are companies who have built a business by designing cards especially for this purpose. There are also mailing services that will send out monthly cards and reminders for a fee.

Do they want to see you

Most of the time when we call on new or prospective accounts we feel like we are bothering them or causing them some type of inconvenience Because of this feeling we sometimes convince ourselves that it is not necessary to make the call and keep on driving by. This attitude has a negative effect on your close.

Just the opposite is true. Most people like to be called on by sales people. Many times their current suppliers are neglecting them, taking the business for granted. By making the call and giving them the attention that may be missing, leaves the door wide open.

Whenever targeting a new account the best approach is to contact the daylights of them. Call them for any reason at all. Write letters. Send clippings. Take an aggressive approach and rush them half to death. It works. There is a tendency for a sales person to let up once they have the business. Give your customer plenty of reasons to buy and the close will be automatic.

Be specific

There is an old saying that one specific is worth a hundred generalities. Being specific demonstrates that you have done your homework.

Don't say "This will increase sales". Say "If you sell just 100 of these per week your profit will be over $12,000 per year". Don't say "This will lower your labor cost". Instead say "This will save you four hours per day in labor cost which will amount to over $7,000 per year in total savings."

The same is true when talking about percentages. The more you can tie it to a dollar amount the more receptive the customer will be. Don't say "This could lower your food cost by one percent". Instead say "this could lower your food cost by at least $10,000 per year, which is a full percentage point".

You can't close on a generality. You can only close on a specific.

Ask for help

A company I was working with needed to sell off a considerable amount of inventory and raise money for their year end P & L statement. It was a fairly large company with sales people covering the entire country. The normal procedure would be to call all the sales people and tell them to call their customers and get the job done. If you have ever been on the selling end of this kind of situation you know how difficult something like this is.

The sales manager took a different approach. Instead of telling each regional manager to get out and sell the extra inventory, he called each one of them and asked for their help. He explained that the company had over produced certain product lines and the company needed to get the inventory down for the end of the year. He suggested to the sales people that they select some of their better customers and ask them to help us out. The results from using this approach was outstanding. It turned out to be the best month the company had in its' entire history. When you ask for help you are giving them a compliment by putting them in a position of power. It is within their power to help you and this makes them feel important.

People always conform

Everyone likes to think of themselves as an individualist, someone who does their own thing. Just the opposite is true in real life. Most everyone likes to belong to a group and do the things everyone else is doing.

If a customer thinks that no one else is using your product or service, you will be hard pressed to get them to be the first. People like to do what others have already done. They like to follow the proven methods that others have already tested.

The best way to use this to our advantage is to put together an impressive list of the customers that are already buying from your company. When you show this list to a prospective customer they will experience a desire to be among the group. Tell them the people on the list are very important and you would like to include them. If you are selling to some of the best companies in town, don't keep it a secret when you are talking to a prospective new account.

Personal interests

Many people are deeply involved in things other than their business. They usually have something in their office that is like an open invitation to ask about it. Many sales people avoid talking about these things because they think it is too obvious, however, just the opposite is true. People attach a great deal of importance to the things in their life other than their work. They add to their overall self image and talking about them gives them a great deal of satisfaction.

I was recently at a mall in Chicago with some time to kill and I saw a computer software booth set up with a display of their programs. I didn't want to sit through a sales pitch, however, I did want to know how much one cost. I approached the sales person and asked for the price and he responded with a question; "What kind of work do you do?" That was all it took. For the next hour we engaged in a conversation about training and if it wasn't for my wife, who came and bailed me out, I might have been the owner of something I had no intention of buying.

Important dates

Besides the obvious dates such as a person's birthday or anniversary, there are other equally important dates.

How many years in business, how many years left on a mortgage, how many years buying from you, how many years with the company. By keeping track of these dates and presenting your customers with an appropriate symbol of recognition, it will do wonders. By looking ahead and planning for important marketing dates far in advance you will always have an edge over the competition. If you list the important marketing dates such as Valentines day, Easter, St Patrick's day, Thanksgiving, etc., and help your customers plan their events you can be sure to capture the business for that period of time.

It is not difficult to put together a system to know when to start talking about an upcoming event or to remind you to congratulate someone. Take 12 envelopes, one for each month, and put notes and reminders in the appropriate month. At the beginning of each month, go through the notes and put them on your calendar.

Ask for advice

The important point to remember when asking for advice is that it must be sincere. The best way to do that is to take notes while they are responding and pay close attention to what they are saying.

Asking for advice is an excellent way to make a person feel important, however, it also has another huge benefit. The advice you get about your company, your products, or whatever you happen to be asking about, may give you an idea that could lead to some substantial new sales.

Some examples of what you can ask advice about: New products. Changes in your service. How to sell another buyer or chef. What they think of certain product features. How can you improve your service.

Customers will find a way to buy from you if they like you. They will also find a way not to buy from you if they don't like you.

Your approach to problems

"You don't understand - my company has some big problems and it makes my job really tough!" Pick up the Sunday paper, go to the classified section and find a job that has no problems. If it is there - they don't need you. A company with problems is a company with opportunities!

A problem is a chance for you to show your best. There are people who spend all their time reinforcing obstacles. Office politics. Perceived defects in the product or service. Impossibly tough competition. Endless personal problems. Unfair commission schedules. We all have problems.

A persistent negative outlook will not only make it difficult for coworkers and supervisors to work with you--it will make it difficult for customers to work with you.

It's common to hear a salesperson complain, "you don't understand how much is expected of us here."

The goals of most sales managers are usually pretty clear-cut: get good results from the staff. If you're not making sales, complaining about everything is only going to compound the problem. Not only will you be wasting valuable time you could be using to talk to new customers, but you'll also lose the perspective you need to identify and resolve the problems you're having.

Many companies have had the experience of having a salesperson perform poorly in a certain territory, complaining that "the market is saturated". Take that person off the territory, put someone else on it, and sales take off.

Usually, the first salesperson focuses on limitations, while the new sales person brings no preconceptions to the territory, and sees fresh opportunities as a result.

The best approach to problems is to become part of the solution. Leaving one company because of problems and going to another is a trade off for new problems. No one likes to be around someone with a negative attitude. Carrying around negativity drags you down and keeps you from moving full speed ahead. A persistent positive attitude can cancel the negative ones.

It takes 4 positive actions or comments to make up for one negative action or comment. Honestly, it takes much more work to remain positive than negative. Negativity in the work environment can spread like a cancer. It starts with one member and quickly moves to other members until the whole office or company is infected. Obstacles will always be a permanent fixture of everyday life, but the bright side is there are ways around them. Satisfaction comes from being victorious over those obstacles.

Years ago I had a customer tell me that he was going to leave and go to a competitor. When I asked why he told me all the things that were wrong with my company. After he told me I realized that I was the one who told him all those things. A good lesson about saying something negative about your own company - it will always come back to bite you.

Follow up: Remove all hope for competitors

My follow up is done so well that my customer can count on me to take care of every detail that will make the process of the sale an enjoyable experience. My follow up starts as soon as I make an initial contact over the phone before the actual visit. I send confirmation letters and recap memos before the sale, during the sale and after the sale. Even if I don't get the sale in the time frame I anticipated, I know that it will only be a matter of time, so my follow up continues with weekly or monthly cards or letters. I stay in touch, keep good records of every contact with the customer, and can put my finger on any piece of information I may need whenever it is necessary.

My 4% improvement objective:

_____

_____

_____

_____

_____

_____

What the entire book series will do for you

Buying all 13 books is like buying a library of 13 powerful coaching sessions that will increase every skill necessary for generating business. Once you experience the seemingly effortless improvement you will understand why there is a picture of Ben Franklin on every 100 dollar bill.

You will learn how to improve relationships, improve management skills, be more productive, generate more customers, negotiate better contracts, open new accounts, earn more profits and create more sales! Results most people only dream about! If you are a sales professional or an entrepreneur this is the perfect program to boost your sales and increase your profits.

Ben Franklin's system

In our fast paced business and personal life today it has become increasingly difficult to set aside time for self development and improving your skills. With every spare minute taken up by reading blogs, logging on to Facebook, following people on Twitter, responding to text messages and emails and constantly talking on your cell phone, there seems to be little, if any, time left for learning new skills. Even the quiet time behind the wheel of your car is no longer available with satellite radio and cell phone coverage in every corner of the country.

Even though this seems like a new problem, distractions have been around forever. Two hundred years ago a man by the name of Ben Franklin had the same problem. He concluded that it was not a matter of distractions as much as a matter of focus. He set out to solve the problem and created the most effective system for self improvement ever invented.

Ben Franklin gives credit for all his success and accomplishments to the implementation of this system for the success he sought after. Despite being born into a poor family and only receiving two years of formal schooling, Ben Franklin became a successful printer, scientist, musician, author and one of the founding fathers of the United States. Ben Franklin is considered to have been one of the most persuasive and successful people in the history of the United States. He was a very skilled sales person, marketer, negotiator and copywriter. Skills that every business owner, professional person, manager and marketer should have.

In the year 1723, Ben Franklin, at the age of seventeen, arrived in Philadelphia without a penny to his name. At age 42, he retired, wealthy, the first self made millionaire in the country. Few people, before or since have ever been as successful as Benjamin Franklin. He gave credit for his many inventions and business successes to his system for self improvement he created when he was 20 years old.

The key to Franklin's success was his drive to constantly improve himself and accomplish his ambitions. In order to accomplish his goal, Franklin developed and committed himself to a personal improvement program that consisted of mastering 13 principles.

When he was seventy-nine years old, Benjamin Franklin wrote more about this idea than anything else that ever happened to him in his entire life. He felt that he owed all his success and happiness to this one thing. Franklin wrote: "I hope, therefore, that some of my descendants may follow the example and reap the benefit."

Since success is developed by performing small and seemingly insignificant acts, you can use this method by reading and putting into practice the 13 skills that will guarantee your success in sales with scientific certainty.

This program takes advantage of Franklin's system and applies it to improving your skills as a sales professional. This program will show you how to dominate your market by first dominating yourself. By focusing on the 13 skills that make up a highly effective and successful sales professional. As these skills are improved your results and sales increases will also show a dramatic improvement.

The goal of going through the program the first time is to increase each skill by only four percent. With the accomplishment of this small improvement in each skill or attitude your overall improvement will be 52%. Those are results most people only dream about. However, you can accomplish this by investing as little as 45 minutes once a week reading one book and then focusing on improving the single skill during the rest of the week. The second week by reading the second book and focusing on that single skill during the week and so on until all 13 weeks are completed.

You can write the single word on the back of your business card and tape it to your dash board as a reminder. You can put this one word on your smart phone as a reminder as well as on your email signature, your Facebook page or you can even have something worthwhile to tweet about. One word, one week, one skill, one "I am" statement, 4% improvement objective and your subconscious mind will receive the message through all the clutter and act on it.

After the first time through the process you can do as Ben Franklin suggests and go through the program a second, third and fourth time. Get your whole sales team on the same page at the same time and you will experience a whirlwind of new excitement and new business. Or get a like minded colleague and join forces with accountability and focus.

Achieve a 52% improvement

Using Franklin's scientific program for learning your objective is to improve 4% in each area over 13 weeks.

1. Attitude Define what you want and go after it.
2. Respect Earn respect-no more comfort zone.
3. Service Help customers build their business.
4. Urgency Be enthusiastic get things done now.
5. Confidence Remove restrictions and limitations.
6. Persistence Keep going and never give up.
7. Planning Get big results by setting big goals.
8. Questions Ask questions that make the sale.
9. Attention Get attention with irresistible offers.
10. Presenting Give reasons why they should buy.
11. Objections Remove every roadblock to the sale.
12. Closing Ask for the order and get paid.
13. Follow up Remove all hope for competitors.

About the author Bob Oros (BobOros.com),

Bob Oros has been a full time speaker and author since 1992 with over 2,000 speaking engagements in all 50 states and several international locations as well as the author of 21 books on sales. Prior to starting his speaking career, Bob served six years in the US Navy as a Communications Specialist and then worked his way from a street sales person to the position of National Sales Manager for a Fortune 200 company.

CSP Award: Bob was awarded the designation of Certified Speaking Professional (CSP) by the National Speakers Association and the International Federation for Professional Speakers. Fewer than 10% of all speakers worldwide qualify for this award.

PWA Member: Bob is a member of the Professional Writers Alliance.

www.ingramcontent.com/pod-product-compliance
Lightning Source LLC
Chambersburg PA
CBHW072258170526
45158CB00003BA/1102